S0-CFF-459

Ahmed Alsoudani
Cut of Time

Published on the occasion of the exhibition *Ahmed Alsoudani*
organized by Marlborough Gallery, New York
May 14 – July 2, 2021

أفق اللوحة، فضاء المعنى (*Painting's Horizon, Meaning's Expanse*)
© 2021 Ali Ahmad Saïd Esber (Adonis)
English translation © Kareem James Abu-Zeid, PhD
Strange Beauty: The Drawings of Ahmed Alsoudani © 2021 Raphael Rubinstein
© 2021 Marlborough Gallery, Inc.

Edition of 1,000

ISBN 978-0-89797-238-3

Ahmed Alsoudani
Cut of Time

With a Foreword by

Adonis

English translation by Kareem James Abu-Zeid, PhD

and

An Essay by

Raphael Rubinstein

www.marlboroughnewyork.com

Table of Contents

Painting's Horizon, Meaning's Expanse

1

"I can see it—how the body of history is torn apart." That's what I almost screamed when I saw the works of Ahmed Alsoudani for the very first time.

I didn't mean the history of times and places, cold and rigid. I meant the history that's alive, explosive, ablaze, the history of the human being in his state of being lost, temporally and spatially, and in his pains and agonies, in his tunnels and labyrinths, where existence appears as a hell burning in the ink, as color and lines, in the brush and its strokes, in the shapes and their relations, and where these elements come together and intensify and coalesce, just as the knife coalesces with the flank.

In all of this, I sensed that the bodies in Ahmed Alsoudani's work are like thoughts, attracting and repelling one another, converging and diverging, while they struggle with the tool of time.

I also sensed that the painting was almost, while I was contemplating it, posing the following question to me:

Why doesn't instinct ever go wrong, whereas reason has been given the freedom to make mistakes? In all of this, I also sensed that the artwork is another path to a vision of the world, in such a way that sight and insight are combined in a vertical gaze, as if it were a probe dropping deeply and distantly into that which is unfathomable.

أفق اللوحة، فضاء المعنى

1

" هُوَذا أرى كيف يتمزّق جسمُ التاريخ ": هكذا كدتُ أصرحُ عندما رأيت، للمرّة الأولى، أعمال أحمد السوداني.

لم أكُن أعني تاريخَ الأيام والأمكنة، باردةً جامدةً. كنت أعني التاريخَ الحيّ، المُتَفَجّر، المُلتَهِب، تاريخَ الكائن البشريّ في ضياعِه، زمانيّاً ومكانيّاً، في آلامِه وتباريحِه، في أنفاقِه ومتاهاتِه، حيث يبدو الوجودُ كمثل جحيم تتأجّج في الجَنّ، لوناً وخطّاً، في الرَّيشَة وضرباتِها، في الأشكال وعلاقاتِها، وحيث تتجمّع هذه العناصرُ وتتكاثفُ وتلتحِمُ كما تلتحِمُ خاصرةٌ وسكّين.

في هذا كلّه، كنت أشعر أنّ الأجسامَ في أعمال أحمد السودانيّ كمثل الأفكار، تتجاذبُ وتتنافر، تتلاقى وتتباعد، فيما تُصارعُ آلةَ الوقت.

كنت كذلك أشعر أنّ اللوحةَ تكادُ أن تطرحَ عليّ، فيما أتأمّلُها هذا السؤال:

لماذا لا تُخطِئُ الغَريزة، بينما أُعطيت للعقل حرّيّةُ الخطأ؟ في هذا كلّه، كنت أشعر أيضاً أنّ العمل الفنّيّ طريقٌ أخرى إلى رؤية العالم على نَحْو يقترنُ فيه البصرُ والبصيرةُ في استشراف عموديّ كأنّه مِسبارٌ يهبطُ عميقاً بعيداً نحْو ما لا قرار له.

2

What does the human body mean, fragmented and divided: a head on one side, and scattered limbs on another side, or on several other sides? What does it mean when its unity has been plundered; when it has been stripped of its coherent structure; and when its natural social function has been disabled? A body like a piece of paper where what was originally written has been effaced, where something else is written afterward. A sheet-body. A trace-body. A body whose identity, as an organizing principle, has been destroyed.

Is not the disabling of the body the disabling of society itself? Is not the disabling of its system the disabling of the system of the image?

And here they are between one color and another: faces that are worn away, bodies that travel in vehicles that are like corridors where time puts on its funereal banquets, feasts for nightmare guests, for remains and rubble, where events and ideas, imagination and vision, all converge to inaugurate a specific aesthetic with new relationships between the material world and the world of creation.

2

ماذا يعني الجسمَ الإنسانّي، مُفكَّكاً مُنشَطِراً: رأساً في جهةٍ، وأطرافاً مُتَناثِرةً، في جهةٍ
أو جهاتٍ أُخرى؟ تُسلَبُ وحدتُهُ، ويُجَرَّدُ من بنيتِهِ المُتَماسكة، وتُعَطَّلُ وظيفتُه الطبيعيّة
الاجتماعيّة؟ جسمٌ كمثل ورقةٍ يُمحى ما كُتبَ عليها بَدئيّاً، ويُكتَبُ ثانيةً عليها شيءٌ آخر،
جسمٌ طِرسٌ. جسمٌ ــ أثرٌ. جسمٌ تتهدّمُ هويّتُه، بوصفِهِ مبدأً مُنظماً.

أليس تعطيلُ الجسمِ تعطيلاً للمجتمعِ نفسهِ؟ أليس تعطيلُ نظامِهِ تعطيلاً
لنظام الصّورةِ؟

وها هي بين لونٍ ولَونٍ، وجوهٌ تتآكَلُ. أجسامٌ تُسافرُ في عرباتٍ كمثل ذهاليزَ يُقيمُ
الوقتُ فيها مأدبتهُ المَأتميّة، والنائمُ لضيوفٍ كوابيس، لأشلاءٍ وأنقاضٍ، حيث تتلاقى
الأحداثُ والأفكارُ المُخيّلةُ والرّؤية، وتنشأُ جماليّةٌ خاصةٌ بعلاقاتٍ جديدةٍ بين عالم
المادّة وعالم الإبداع.

3

History in Ahmed Alsoudani's work is a meaning-body: the painting is a new formation of this body, another depiction of its ruptures, and another meaning of meaning. This is how the single body becomes many. How the organs become colors. How the blood becomes quill and ink—in a plural singular, in colors-visions. And this is his painting: image word voice intonation movement leaping repose tension crawling climbing groping retreat attack.

On the wall of time the same painting is hung, beyond the shadow and beyond the sun: between them. This is how it appears sometimes, as if it were a dome for the wind, and at other times as if it were a chariot of planets preparing to journey. A world ever-present before us—yet in a continuous state of absence. As if the moment were a flame, as if the painting were moving around within this flame and not emerging from it except by turning into a garment for the future.

This is how the painting appears, as if it were space for the one that is many. Space for the many that are composed of disparate elements, and for relationships that distinguish among these elements, and for individual aspects that correspond to these relationships.

التّاريخ عند أحمد السوداني معنى ـ جسمٌ : اللوحة تشكيلٌ جديدٌ لهذا الجسم، وتصويرٌ
آخر لتمزّقاته. ومعنى آخر للمعنى. هكذا يصبح الجسمُ الواحدُ كثيراً. وتصبح الأعضاءُ
ألواناً. ويصبح الدّمُ ريشةً وحبراً ـ في مفردِ جَمْعٍ، وفي ألوانٍ ـ رؤًى. وها هي لوحته
صورةٌ كلمةِ صوتٍ نبرةٍ حركةِ قفزٍ استرخاءٍ توتّرٍ زحفٍ تسلّقٍ تنسّلٍ تلمّسٍ انكفاءٍ هجومٍ.

على حائط الوقتِ تُعَلِّق اللوحةُ نفسَها، خارجَ الظلِّ وخارجَ الشّمس: بينهما. هكذا تبدو
أحياناً كأنّها مُقنعةٌ للرّيح. وحيناً كأنّها عربةٌ لكواكبَ تتهيّأ للسّفر. عالمٌ دائمُ الحضور
أمامنا ـ لكن في حالةٍ متواصلةٍ من الغياب. كأنّ اللحظةَ لهبٌ، وكأنّ اللوحةَ تتنقّلُ في
هذا اللهب ولا تخرج منه إلّا في تحوّلِها قميصاً للمستقبل.

هكذا تبدو اللوحةُ كأنّها فضاءٌ للواحد الكثير. فضاء كثرةٍ تتكوّنُ من عناصرَ مُتباينة.
وعلاقاتٍ تُمَيِّز فيما بين هذه العناصر. وفراداتٍ تتطابقُ مع هذه العلاقات.

4

The aesthetic dimension is structurally connected to the revelatory-epistemic dimension.

History in its current embodiments is a deep hollow that is both fathomless and near at hand, and from it the painting emerges in a robe of the imagination and in an undulation of color.

It emerges in a paradox-question:
> No solution, no answer, but rather insight and investigation.

The where and the no-where exchange their places and times, where the painting appears as a play in layers and elements that overlap and interact, culturally and emotionally and aesthetically. A play on whose stage the hide of history is cracking, while the skin of space is stained with the gasping of its rubble.

The days don the external husk, while the core sinks to the bottom of the imagination. And this imagination penetrates all layers, as the barriers before them migrate, so as to settle in the dream's embrace.

Each painting is a kind of strange migration surrounded by a tragic aesthetic, internally and externally, a migration that requires a reconsideration of all things, even of the meaning of "country-homeland." And it invites you to repeat the old and oft-quoted saying: "No country has more of a claim to you than any other, and the best country is the one that embraces you."

In this way, reality in Ahmed Alsoudani's vision appears neither to be what it is, nor to be anything other than what it is.

4

البعد الجماليّ يقترن بنيوياً بالبعد الكشفيّ المعرفيّ.

التاريخ في تجسّداته الرّاهنة غَورٌ عميق بعيدٌ قريب، تخرج منه اللوحة في ثوب المُخَيِّلة وفي تموّج اللون.

تخرج في إشكال ـ سؤال:
لا حلَّ، لا جواب، بل استبصارٌ واستقصاء.

الأينُ واللا أينُ يتبادلان مكانيهما وزمانيهما. حيث تبدو اللوحةُ مسرحاً في مستويات وعناصرَ تتداخلُ وتتصادى، ثقافياً وانفعالياً وجمالياً. مسرحٌ يتشقَّقُ على خَشبتِه جلدُ التاريخ، وتتبقّع بشرةُ الفضاء بلُهاثِ أنقاضه.

القشرةُ ما تلبسه الأيّام، واللّبابُ يترسَّبُ في قاع المُخَيِّلة. وهذه تخترق الطبقات كلّها حيث تهاجِرُ الحواجز أمامها، لكي تستقرّ في أحضان الحلم.

كلُّ لوحةٍ نوعٌ من هجرةٍ غريبةٍ تحفُّ بها جماليّةٌ فاجعةٌ، داخليّة وخارجيّة، هجرة تفرض إعادة النّظر في كلِّ شيءٍ، حتى في معنى " البلاد ـ الوطن ". وتدعوك إلى تكرار القول المأثور: " ليس بلدٌ أَحَقَّ بك من بلدٍ. خيرُ البلادِ ما حَمَلَكَ ".

هكذا يبدو الواقع في رؤية أحمد السودانيّ أنّه لا هُوَ هُوَ. ولا هُوَ غيرُ ما هُوَ.

5

Alsoudani inaugurates a new aesthetic that I call the aesthetic of intensification: the greater world, enclosed within the lesser world.

It is an aesthetic of forming new relationships between body and body, signal and signal, energy and energy, and between light and light. The canvas is a bed for the social-cultural body, in terms of movement and formation and color, suffering and rupture—on another horizon of the dynamism of formation and genesis.

And the painting here is a herald that wanders about like a prophecy in the desert of time, or in the belly of a cosmic whale. And color, here, appears as if it were not the stroke of a brush so much as the stroke of fate. It is as if the clouds were living in tents built by thunderbolts, or as if the mountains and plains and forests were tents built by thunderbolts, or were trading places in the geography of light, and in the maps of the wind.

Truly, life is a spark, and painting is a flame.

Adonis
(Paris, 1st of March, 2021)

Translated from the Arabic by Kareem James Abu-Zeid, PhD

يبتكرُ السّودانيّ جماليّةً جديدة أسمّيها جماليّة التّكثيف: العالَمُ الأكبرِ مُنطوياً في العالم الأصغر.

إنها جماليّةُ تكوينٍ لعلاقاتٍ جديدة بين الجسم والجسم، الإشارة والإشارة، الطّاقة والطّاقة، وبين الضّوء والضّوء، القماشةُ سريرٌ، فراشٌ، للجسم الاجتماعيّ ـ الثّقافيّ، حركةٌ وتشكيلاً ولوناً، عذاباً وتمَزُّقاً ـ في أفقٍ آخر لحرَكيّةِ التّشكيل والتّكوين.

واللوحةُ هنا نذيرٌ يتشرّدُ كمثل نبوّةٍ في صحراء الزّمن. أو في جوف حوتٍ كونيّ. ويبدو اللونُ هنا كأنّه ليس ضربة الفرشاةِ بقدر ما هو ضربةُ المَصير. كما لو أنّ الغيومَ تعيش في خِيامٍ تبنيها الصّواعق. أو كأنّ الجبالَ والسّهولَ والغاباتِ خيامٌ تبنيها الصّواعق. أو كأنّ الجبالَ والسّهولَ والغاباتِ تتبادل مواقعَها في جغرافيةٍ الضّوء. وفي خرائط الرّيح.

حقاً، الحياةُ شرارةٌ، واللّوحة لَهَبٌ.

أدونيس
(باريس، أول مارس، 2021)

Ahmed Alsoudani, *Cut of Time 11,* 2020, acrylic and pen on paper, 14 x 11 in. | 35.6 x 27.9 cm

Strange Beauty: The Drawings of Ahmed Alsoudani

One of the ways to recognize an artist of real substance is to ask whether they create a distinctive world. As we encounter each successive work, does another portion of a vivid and seemingly infinite realm reveal itself? Do we feel that the artist is both cosmogenic and cartographic, simultaneously creating a new world and mapping it out? Such universe-creating works come in a variety of modes: they can be pictorial (late Philip Guston, for instance), or abstract (Stanley Whitney's ever-refreshed combinatorial grids) or, sometimes, abstract and pictorial all at once (the florid gestural gardens of Joan Mitchell). This third hybrid approach is the one favored by Ahmed Alsoudani, a cosmogenic painter whose thronging, tumultuous compositions don't so much erase the differences between the representational and the abstract as supercharge them into the most intense versions of themselves and set them loose to see what happens.

This modal intensity contributes to the chaotic nature of the realm that Alsoudani paints into existence with each canvas. His is not a peaceable kingdom, it is, rather, a zone of struggle and tension in which every element seems to be attacking not only its neighbors but even itself. When we lend our gaze to these pictures it is as if we are hurling ourselves into battle. The atmosphere of conflict and threatened violence conveyed by Alsoudani's paintings is heightened by the sheer quantity of event they contain. There is so much turmoil, so much explosive energy in these paintings that they constantly threaten to burst the banks of the stretched canvas. As visions of barely controllable chaos they belong to an artistic lineage that includes such early-20th-century works as Umberto Boccioni's *The City Rises* (1910), Carlo Carrà's *Funeral of the Anarchist Galli* (1910-11) and George Grosz's *The Funeral* (1917-1918). There are also strong connections to the baroque late-1930s phase of Surrealist painting in works such as André Masson's *Tauromachie* (1937) and *In the Tower of Sleep* (1938), and Max Ernst's *L'ange du foyer* and *La conversion du feu* (both 1937), four turbulent paintings created as the artists watched much of Europe succumb to the forces of Fascism. Reaching back further into art history, we can see echoes in Alsoudani's work of the sinuous torments in the Laocoön Group and in the gruesome beauty of Titian's late masterpiece *The Flaying of Marsyas* (1570-76). And yet, for all these grim precedents, Alsoudani's paintings and drawings are beautiful works. Strangely beautiful, perhaps, uncomfortably beautiful, but beautiful all the same. What did Rilke say in the *Duino Elegies*? "Beauty is nothing but the beginning of a terror which we are barely able to endure because it serenely disdains to destroy us."[1] If the cohabitation of beauty and terror has often been a defining feature

André Masson, *In the Tower of Sleep*, 1938, oil on canvas, 32 x 39 ½ in.. | 81.3 x 100.3 cm

1. Rilke, Rainer Maria, J. B. Leishman, and Stephen Spender. *Duino Elegies*.
   London: Hogarth Press, 1963.

Max Ernst, *L'ange du foyer*, 1937, oil on canvas, 44 ¾ x 57 ½ in. | 114 x 146 cm

of Alsoudani's war-haunted paintings, the proportions of these two states have changed rather dramatically in the work he has been making since the onset of the COVID-19 pandemic. Finding himself temporarily living outside of New York City and working in a small domestic space rather than in his large Chelsea studio, the artist did what artists have always done: find ways to keep on working, to continue creating. For Alsoudani, this meant turning to a much smaller scale and working with acrylic paint and ink on paper.

Max Ernst, *La conversion du feu*, 1937, oil on canvas, 15 x 21 ½ in. | 38 x 54.6 cm

Not surprisingly, the shift in scale and materials had consequences for the form and content of the new work. While never fully figurative, Alsoudani's paintings have long been filled with imagery evocative of body parts: heads, limbs, torsos, skulls, bones and sexual organs, as well as fragments of furniture and architecture and stray geometric elements. These body parts aren't necessarily human—they constitute a kind of inter-species carnival—but they pulse with organic life and are rendered in emphatic three-dimensionality. In the recent drawings the figurative allusions are less pervasive, which makes room for a bolder, efflorescent gesturalism, and beauty seems to be gaining an advantage over terror. At first glance it can look as if Alsoudani has leapt from the Surrealist amalgam of automatism and illusionism of the 1930s—typified by Max Ernst's *L'Ange du Foyer* (1937)—to the fully gestural style of Abstract Expressionism in the late 1940s. But as we look more closely this art-historical analogy begins to fall apart. While it's absolutely true that the new work on paper relies more on gesture and less on figural form than the preceding paintings, illusionism is still present, we just have to look a little harder to find it.

In fact, this process of discovery is one of the great pleasures of Alsoudani's drawings. After grasping the composition as an expression of sheer energy, registering the fountain-like jets of color as they describe arcs, zigzags, sinuous curves and sudden splatters, our looking slows down to take in the details. It turns out they are many, and often

André Masson, *Tauromachie*, 1937, oil on canvas, 32 x 39 ½ in. | 81.3 x 100.3 cm

incredibly subtle and diminutive. We notice how the artist uses a fine-pointed pen to often treat nearly every inch, every shape, in a drawing with crosshatching, with sets of feathery lines, with clumps of precise scribbling, with intricate patterning that evokes natural phenomenon such as fish scales, reptile skins and peacock feathers. At times tiny decorative motifs function like tattoos that have been stained into the "flesh" of the shapes. Also activating the compositions are rivers and pools of black that dramatically punctuate the swirling colors. Occasionally he will add curious imagery like a bracelet of tiny orbs wrapped around a shard-like dirt-brown gesture or a row of short arcing lines that seem sewn into a shape like a surgeon's sutures.

The more we study these drawings, the more we appreciate their intricate delicacy of detail. Working simultaneously on a number of drawings, Alsoudani achieves this effect in phases. First, using a restricted palette, he will lay quick gestures onto a dozen or so sheets of watercolor paper. Then, switching from paintbrush to pen, he will go back into each drawing, making countless additions and alterations. Often he will also add more gestures in a growing range of colors, and thin out his colors to allow the texture of the paper to play a role. Throughout, the gestural marks serve as the armature upon which the drawing is built, but the process is more organic than architectural. Details accumulate on the brushstroke shapes the way ivy grows on a tree or barnacles on a rock, and although the process is additive, sometimes there is a suggestion of parts being worn away or otherwise broken up, as if by erosion or some other form of entropy. Another distinctive feature of the drawings is how many of the shapes are so weirdly elongated that they might be harboring an anamorphic image, like the famous skull in Holbein's *The Ambassadors* (1533). You almost want to try looking at them from extreme angles in the hope that some recognizable image will emerge.

Here might be a good place to wonder about how and why so many shapes in Alsoudani's work suggest bones and skulls. The "how" has

Carroll Dunham, *Tall Birch*, 1983, mixed media on birch, 76 x 48 in. | 193 x 122 cm

something to do with the artist's penchant for depicting hollow shapes, for adding shadows that turn a gesture into a fragile container that might be the skull of a bird or just as easily the fragment of some ancient vessel. As to why, there is a sense of fragility inherent in all of Alsoudani's work, as if there were forces unleashed in the paintings that have the capacity to if not destroy then to disrupt and deterritorialize everything they touch. In order to not be destroyed by this invisible power, the shapes in his work have adapted themselves to allow a maximum of flow and pliability; they let this wind of disruption flow through as well as around themselves; nothing is solid.

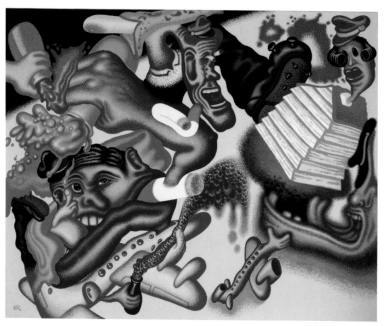

Peter Saul, *Stupid Argument*, 2010, acrylic and oil on canvas, 78 x 96 in. | 198.1 x 243.8 cm

A related motif are the orifices that Alsoudani loves to insert into his shapes, holes (sometimes with things entering or exiting them) that seem to have erupted on the skins of the intertwined forms. If some of his paintings tremble with unraveling violence—not surprising given his youth in war-torn Iraq—others choreograph orgies of polymorphous eroticism. With their pulsating vaginal and phallic motifs, some of Alsoudani's paintings rival Carroll Dunham's Surrealist-inspired paintings on wood panel of the early 1980s for their foregrounding of primal sexual energy. But if there are clear affinities between these two artists, the distinctions are just as sharp: Dunham draws on the vernacular spirit of comics and cartooning, which isn't a factor in Alsoudani's work, and his imagery, so frequently fecal, revels in the abject and the soiled, while the forms in Alsoudani's work feel stripped as clean as the skeleton in the midst of a desert. It's also interesting to compare Alsoudani's work with that of Peter Saul, another painter who found ways to reanimate the legacy of Surrealism. Although Saul's work is far more explicitly figurative than Alsoudani's, both artists relish filling every inch of their canvases with riotous, multidirectional forms.

What are we to make of the radical duality of these drawings, which marry the instantaneous gesture to the meticulously etched detail? Here, any notion of stylistic purity is discarded. The drawings refuse to be categorized. They are neither exclusively abstract nor representational. Instead, they deploy what Clement Greenberg called "homeless representation," which he defined as "plastic and descriptive painterliness that is applied to abstract ends."[2] For Greenberg this wasn't a desirable thing and he lamented its appearance in 1950s paintings by De Kooning and Guston. It's been a long time, thankfully, since the purity of abstraction has been a matter of concern. On the contrary, it could be argued that "homeless representation" has been an indispensable tool for some of the most compelling painters of recent decades, artists such as Amy Sillman, Laura Owens, Lydia Dona and Carrie Moyer. So, too, is Alsoudani's work grounded in the cross-fertilization of representation and abstraction.

---

2. Clement Greenberg, "After Abstract Expressionism," Art International, October 1962, reprinted in Clement Greenberg, The Collected Essays and Criticism, vol. 4, ed. John O'Brian, University of Chicago Press, Chicago and London, 1993, p. 124.

Alsoudani's rejection of the representation/abstraction binary becomes the ground for a larger challenge in his work to binary thinking in general and its attendant hierarchies. Instead, Alsoudani embraces a rhizomatic approach, to borrow a well-known term from philosopher Gilles Deleuze for whom the horizontally spreading multiplicity of rhizomatic plants like bamboo was a preferable model of thinking, indeed of society, to the vertical arborescent structure of the tree. We can understand the interconnected relationship between Alsoudani's broad brushstrokes and the families of miniature ink lines attached to them as rhizomatic, and also the way in which each drawing presents us with a constellation of elements that float freely in space, without roots, without top and bottom, without anchor, disoriented or constantly reoriented. In many ways, Alsoudani's work was already perfectly suited to a radically destabilized moment such as the one we are in now, and even as he adapted to the isolation and restricted quarters of pandemic life, he already had a painterly vocabulary at hand that was flexible and free enough to find its way into the new types of spaces that are opening up all around us. ∎

Raphael Rubinstein

Plates

Cut of Time 1, 2020

acrylic and pen on paper
11 x 14 in. | 27.9 x 35.6 cm

Cut of Time 2, 2020

acrylic and pen on paper
11 x 14 in. | 27.9 x 35.6 cm

***Cut of Time 3,* 2020**

acrylic and pen on paper
11 x 14 in. | 27.9 x 35.6 cm

Cut of Time 4, 2020

acrylic and pen on paper
11 x 14 in. | 27.9 x 35.6 cm

Cut of Time 5, 2020

acrylic and pen on paper
14 x 11 in. | 35.6 x 27.9 cm

***Cut of Time 6,* 2020**

acrylic and pen on paper
11 x 14 in. | 27.9 x 35.6 cm

***Cut of Time 7,* 2020**

acrylic and pen on paper
11 x 14 in. | 27.9 x 35.6 cm

Cut of Time 8, *2020*

acrylic and pen on paper
11 x 14 in. | 27.9 x 35.6 cm

Cut of Time 9, 2020
acrylic and pen on paper
11 x 14 in. | 27.9 x 35.6 cm

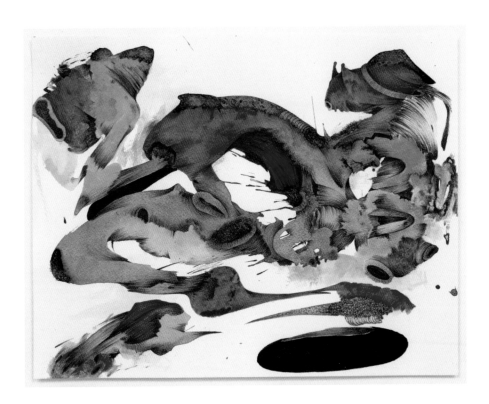

Cut of Time 10, 2020

acrylic and pen on paper
11 x 14 in. | 27.9 x 35.6 cm

Cut of Time 11, 2020

acrylic and pen on paper
11 x 14 in. | 27.9 x 35.6 cm

***Cut of Time 12,* 2020**

acrylic and pen on paper
14 x 11 in. | 35.6 x 27.9 cm

***Cut of Time 13,* 2020**

acrylic and pen on paper
11 x 14 in. | 27.9 x 35.6 cm

Cut of Time 14, 2020

acrylic and pen on paper
11 x 14 in. | 27.9 x 35.6 cm

***Cut of Time 15,* 2020**

acrylic and pen on paper
11 x 14 in. | 27.9 x 35.6 cm

***Cut of Time 16*, 2020**

acrylic and pen on paper
11 x 14 in. | 27.9 x 35.6 cm

Cut of Time 17, **2020**

acrylic and pen on paper
11 x 14 in. | 27.9 x 35.6 cm

Cut of Time 18, 2020

acrylic and pen on paper
11 x 14 in. | 27.9 x 35.6 cm

***Cut of Time 19,* 2020**

acrylic and pen on paper
11 x 14 in. | 27.9 x 35.6 cm

***Cut of Time 20,* 2020**

acrylic and pen on paper
11 x 14 in. | 27.9 x 35.6 cm

Cut of Time 21, **2020**

acrylic and pen on paper
11 x 14 in. | 27.9 x 35.6 cm

***Cut of Time 22*, 2020**

acrylic and pen on paper
11 x 14 in. | 27.9 x 35.6 cm

Cut of Time 23, 2020

acrylic and pen on paper
11 x 14 in. | 27.9 x 35.6 cm

***Cut of Time 24*, 2020**

acrylic and pen on paper
11 x 14 in. | 27.9 x 35.6 cm

Cut of Time 25, 2020

acrylic and pen on paper
14 x 11 in. | 35.6 x 27.9 cm

Cut of Time 26, 2020

acrylic and pen on paper
11 x 14 in. | 27.9 x 35.6 cm

Cut of Time 27, 2020

acrylic and pen on paper
11 x 14 in. | 27.9 x 35.6 cm

Cut of Time 28, 2020

acrylic and pen on paper
14 x 11 in. | 35.6 x 27.9 cm

***Cut of Time 29,* 2020**

acrylic and pen on paper
11 x 14 in. | 27.9 x 35.6 cm

Cut of Time 30, 2020

acrylic and pen on paper
11 x 14 in. | 27.9 x 35.6 cm

About Ahmed Alsoudani

Ahmed Alsoudani was born in 1975 in Baghdad, Iraq. From an early age, he nurtured a pronounced interest in drawing and reading. With access to a home library with a diverse collection assembled by his older brother's friend, Alsoudani spent most of his youth reading, developing an especial fascination with Russian literature, which opened his eyes to the world and would later profoundly influence his art practice.

In early 1995, Alsoudani left his home for Damascus, Syria, where he lived among Iraqi and Arab artists and poets for four years. These deeply enriching relationships allowed him to clearly set his artistic objectives. He began to read about art in-depth and developed more serious understandings of drawing and painting. During this time, his growing desire to become an artist and search for a better life led him to the United States in 1998.

After spending his first year in Washington, D.C., Alsoudani arrived in Portland, Maine in 1999, where he completed his first academic study at Maine College of Art (MECA) from 2001 until 2005. During his junior year, Alsoudani was accepted to Yale Norfolk Summer School of Art, a program established in 1948 for young undergraduate art majors, and where Philip Guston and Willem de Kooning had once taught and served as visiting artists. While Alsoudani completed the program, other visiting artists included Kiki Smith and Dana Schutz.

In the summer of 2006, the Skowhegan School of Painting and Sculpture awarded Alsoudani with his second residency where he worked alongside fellow visiting artists Joan Jonas and Nicole Eisenman. Working for the first time in his own studio, Alsoudani experienced life as a full-time artist for nine weeks, propelling him further towards his goal of becoming a painter.

Alsoudani was accepted to The Yale School of Art in the fall of 2006, where he would pursue his Master of Fine Arts in Painting. For two years, the artist studied with Peter Halley, Robert Storr, Mel Bochner, Caroll Dunham, and Sam Messer, all of whom greatly helped him shape his thoughts and artistic practice.

After graduating from Yale in 2008, Alsoudani moved to Berlin, eager to experience the German art scene first-hand after studying German art and literature during his undergraduate studies. While residing in Berlin, the artist had solo exhibitions at Goff + Rosenthal in Berlin and Robert Goff Gallery in New York. His work was also featured at *Unveiled: New Art from the Middle East* at Saatchi Gallery in London in 2009, which brought the emerging artist increased attention.

Alsoudani returned to the United States in the fall of 2009, where he settled in New York City's Soho neighborhood, a century-old hub for artists, and established his studio in Chelsea, amidst its plethora of contemporary art galleries.

In 2011, Alsoudani represented Iraq in the 54th Venice Biennale, the country's first presentation in 35 years. At the same time, his work was featured in *The World Belongs to You* at the Pinault Collection's Palazzo Grassi, Venice. The same year, Alsoudani was featured in *Told / Untold / Retold* at the Arab Museum of Modern Art, Doha, Qatar and mounted a solo exhibition at Haunch of Venison in London.

In 2012, Alsoudani mounted his first solo museum exhibition at the Wadsworth Atheneum Museum of Art in Hartford, Connecticut. The same year, the artist held his second exhibition with Haunch of Venison in New York, as well as a solo presentation with L&M Arts in Los Angeles, California.

In February 2013, Marlborough Chelsea organized the group exhibition *Ahmed Alsoudani, Francis Bacon, Philip Guston, Paula Rego*. The following month, the artist's second solo museum exhibition *Redacted* opened at the Phoenix Museum of Art, Phoenix, Arizona, which subsequently traveled to the Portland Museum of Art, Portland, Maine. Another solo exhibition opened at Veneklasen/Werner, Berlin in September of that year. Gladstone Gallery mounted the artist's next solo exhibition in the fall of 2014 in New York. Alsoudani's work was later featured at *Maine Collected* at the Bates College Museum of Art in 2015.

In 2017 Marlborough London presented Alsoudani's first solo exhibition with the gallery, followed by a second solo exhibition at Marlborough New York in the fall of 2018.

In December of 2018, Alsoudani was featured in *Artists in Exile: Expressions of Loss and Hope* at The Yale University Art Gallery alongside Max Beckmann, Arshile Gorky, and R. B. Kitaj, among others. Alsoudani was also included in the 2018 exhibition, *Chaos and Awe: Paintings for the 21st Century,* at the Frist Art Museum in Nashville, Tennessee. The exhibition then traveled to the Chrysler Museum of Art, Norfolk, Virginia in 2019.

Alsoudani's forthcoming museum solo exhibition will open in November 2021 at the Fabric Workshop and Museum, Philadelphia, Pennsylvania, following a two-year residency there.

Selected Public Collections

Bates College Museum of Art, Lewiston, Maine
Columbus Museum of Art, Columbus, Ohio
Mead Art Museum, Amherst College, Amherst, Massachusetts
Phoenix Museum of Art, Phoenix, Arizona
Pinault Foundation, Paris, France
Portland Museum of Art, Portland, Maine
The Saatchi Gallery, London, United Kingdom
The Yale University Art Gallery, New Haven, Connecticut
Virginia Museum of Fine Arts, Richmond, Virginia
Wadsworth Atheneum Museum of Art, Hartford, Connecticut

About Adonis

Born Ali Ahmad Saïd Esber in 1930 in Syria, Adonis is an internationally renowned poet, essayist and theoretician of Arab poetics. He is referred to as "the greatest living poet of the Arab world" and "the grand old man of poetry, secularism and free speech in the Arab world." Adopting the pen name Adonis in the 1940s, he has been writing for more than 75 years and has published more than fifty works of poetry, criticism, essays, and translations, all written in Arabic. Much of his work has been translated to English, French, Chinese, Spanish, Italian, Swedish, and German, among other languages. His modernist influence on Arabic poetry is often compared to that of T. S. Eliot on Anglophone poetry.

Adonis has won numerous awards, including the highest French honor of Chevalier of the Légion d'Honneur (2012). Other accolades include the Grand Prize of the Biennale Internationale de la Poésie (Liège, 1986), Goethe Prize (Frankfurt, 2011), and the US PEN/Nabokov International Literature Lifetime Achievement Award (2017), among others.

Adonis has been living and working in Paris since 1986.

About Raphael Rubinstein

Raphael Rubinstein is a New York-based writer and art critic whose numerous books include *The Miraculous* (Paper Monument, 2014), *A Geniza* (Granary Books, 2015) and monographs on Shirley Jaffe (Flammarion, 2014), Albert Oehlen (Hetzler/Nahmad Contemporary, 2020) and Guillermo Kuitca (Lund Humphries, 2020). His poetry has appeared in, among other places, *Grand Street, Fence* and *Harper's Magazine* and in *Best American Poetry 2015*. From 1997 to 2007, he was a senior editor at *Art in America,* where he continues to be a contributing editor. Since 2008 he has been Professor of Critical Studies at the University of Houston School of Art. His column of micro-narratives "The Miraculous: New York" appears monthly in *The Brooklyn Rail.* Chapters from *Libraries of Sand,* his work-in-progress about the Egyptian-Jewish poet Edmond Jabès, have appeared in *Bomb Magazine, Jacket2* and *The Fortnightly Review.*

Staff Directory

Marlborough New York
545 West 25th Street
New York, NY 10001
United States Of America
+1 212 541 4900

Douglas Kent Walla, CEO   dkwalla@marlboroughgallery.com

Sebastian Sarmiento, Director   sebastian@marlboroughgallery.com
Nicole Sisti, Assistant to Sebastian Sarmiento   sisti@marlboroughgallery.com

Diana Burroughs, Director   dburroughs@marlboroughgallery.com
Ren Pan, Assistant to Diana Burroughs   pan@marlboroughgallery.com

Alexa Burzinski, Associate Director   burzinski@marlboroughgallery.com

Meghan Boyle Kirtley, Administrator   boyle@marlboroughgallery.com
Greg O'Connor, Comptroller   greg@marlboroughgallery.com
Dibomba Kazadi, Bookkeeper   kazadi@marlboroughgallery.com

Amy Caulfield, Registrar   caulfield@marlboroughgallery.com
Bianca Clark, Registrar   clark@marlboroughgallery.com

Lukas Hall, Archivist   hall@marlboroughgallery.com
Marissa Moxley, Archivist   moxley@marlboroughgallery.com

Sarah Gichan, Gallery Assistant   gichan@marlboroughgallery.com

John Willis, Warehouse Manager   willis@marlboroughgallery.com

Anthony Nici, Master Crater   mnywarehouse@marlboroughgallery.com
Jeff Serino, Preparator   mnywarehouse@marlboroughgallery.com
Peter Park, Preparator   park@marlboroughgallery.com
Robert Richburg, Preparator   richburg@marlboroughgallery.com
Matt Castillo, Preparator   mnywarehouse@marlboroughgallery.com

Marlborough Fine Art (London)
6 Albemarle Street
Mayfair
London W1S 4BY
United Kingdom
+44 20 7629 5161

John Erle-Drax, Chairman
erle-drax@marlboroughgallery.com

Mary Miller, Director
miller@marlboroughgallery.com

Geoffrey Parton, Director
parton@marlboroughgallery.com

Frankie Rossi, Managing Director
rossi@marlboroughgallery.com

Deborah Lowe, Accounts Assistant
lowe@marlboroughgallery.com

Angela Trevatt,
Senior Bookkeeper/ Finance and Administrative
trevatt@marlboroughgallery.com

Joe Balfour, Head of Graphics
balfour@marlboroughgallery.com

Jessica Draper, Sales Director
draper@marlboroughgallery.com

Laura Langeluddecke,
Executive Assistant to Directors and Researcher
langeluddecke@marlboroughgallery.com

Michael Pollard, Fine Art Registrar
pollard@marlboroughgallery.com

Kate Chipperfield, Sales / Graphics Registrar
chipperfield@marlboroughgallery.com

Harry Coday, Gallery Assistant Digital
coday@marlboroughgallery.com

Will Wright, Associate Director
wright@marlboroughgallery.com

Galería Marlborough Madrid
Orfila, 5
28010 Madrid
Spain
+34 91 319 1414

Anne Barthe, Sales Director	abarthe@gameriamarlborough.com
Belén Herrera Ottino, Sales Director	bherrera@galeriamarlborough.com
Claudia Manzano, Sales	cmanzano@galeriamarlborough.com
Nerea Pérez, Press, Auctions	nperez@galeriamarlborough.com
Nieves Rubiño, Director of Finance, Legal and HR	nrubino@galeriamarlborough.com
Germán Lucas, Finance Assistant	glucas@galeriamarlborough.com
Cynthia González, Registrar	cgonzalez@galeriamarlborough.com
Jara Herranz, Catalogues, Archives	jherranz@galeriamarlborough.com
Noemí Morena, Reception	nmorena@galeriamarlborough.com
Fermín Rosado, Warehouse	frosado@galeriamarlborough.com
Juan García, Warehouse	jgarcia@galeriamarlborough.com

Galería Marlborough Barcelona
C/ Enric Granados, 68
08008 Barcelona
+34 93 467 44 54

Mercedes Ros, Director, Sales, Public Relations	mros@galeriamarlborough.com
Laura Rodríguez, Registrar, Press, Sales, Reception	lrodriguez@galeriamarlborough.com
Ester García, Catalogues, Press, Reception	eguntin@galeriamarlborough.com

Photo Credits

In order of appearance:

All works by Ahmed Alsoudani: © Ahmed Alsoudani.
Photography: Pierre Le Hors.

André Masson (French, 1896-1987), *In the Tower of Sleep,* 1938, oil on canvas, 32 x 39 1/2 in. (81.3 x 100.3 cm). 35 1/4 x 42 3/4 x 2 5/16 in. (89.5 x 108.6 x 5.9 cm). The Baltimore Museum of Art: Bequest of Saidie A. May, BMA 1951.329. Photography: Mitro Hood. © 2021 Artists Rights Society (ARS), New York / ADAGP, Paris.

Max Ernst (German, 1891-1976), *L'ange du foyer,* 1937, oil on canvas, 44 3/4 x 57 1/2 in. (114 x 146 cm). Private collection. © 2021 Artists Rights Society (ARS), New York / ADAGP, Paris. Courtesy Art Resource, New York.

Max Ernst (German, 1891-1976), *La conversion du feu,* 1937, oil on canvas, 15 x 21 1/2 in. (38 x 54.6 cm). Private collection. © 2021 Artists Rights Society (ARS), New York / ADAGP, Paris. Courtesy Sotheby's, New York.

André Masson (French, 1896-1987), *Tauromachie,* 1937, oil on canvas, 32 x 39 1/2 in. (81.3 x 100.3 cm). Framed: 33 1/2 x 41 x 2 in. (85.1 x 104.1 x 5.1 cm). The Baltimore Museum of Art: The Cone Collection, formed by Dr. Claribel Cone and Miss Etta Cone of Baltimore, Maryland, BMA 1950.349. Photography: Mitro Hood. © 2021 Artists Rights Society (ARS), New York / ADAGP, Paris.

Carroll Dunham (American, b. 1949), *Tall Birch,* 1983, mixed media on birch, 76 x 48 in. (193 x 122 cm). Private collection. © Carroll Dunham. Courtesy the artist and Gladstone Gallery, New York and Brussels.

Peter Saul (American, b. 1934), *Stupid Argument,* 2010, acrylic and oil on canvas, 78 x 96 in. (198.1 x 243.8 cm). Private collection. Photography: Kevin Noble. © 2021 Peter Saul / Artists Rights Society (ARS), New York. Courtesy Corbett vs. Dempsey, Chicago.

Design: Sydney Smith
Editors: Alexa Burzinski, Lukas Hall, Marissa Moxley,
Sebastian Sarmiento, Nicole Sisti

Edition of 1,000
Printed in China by Permanent Press

$14.95
ISBN 978-0-89797-238-3
51495>

9 780897 972383